Western Austra

Western Australia occupies one-third of the Australian continent. From the mangroves and monsoon plains of the Kimberley to the towering Karri forests and rugged granite headlands of the Great Southern, this largest State is packed full of natural wonders.

Much of the interior is desert, and the soils of the well-watered south-west corner are not rich in plant nutrients. Yet, every springtime, especially after good winter rains, the red aridlands are carpeted with wildflowers and the coastal plains and sandy heathlands are ablaze with blossoms of all colours, shapes and textures. Many of Western Australia's approximately 8000 species of wildflowers are found nowhere else in the world.

It is possible to travel through Western Australia discovering unspoiled beaches, rugged ranges where few travellers penetrate and bushland free of the hand of humankind. It is also possible to journey from place to place, savouring the best of accommodation, wonderful food and the warmest of hospitality. Perth, the capital city, and its companion port, Fremantle, on the broad banks of the Swan River, are modern centres of commerce and industry in which magnificent restaurants and sophisticated entertainment can be found. Even the smallest country towns have their own welcoming lifestyles.

This is a State that owes its prosperity to vast mineral deposits, agriculture and the pastoral industry. It is also rich in culture and human resources. Its people are of many ethnic origins and they have forged a self-reliant society that enjoys its natural heritage and is always happy to share its good fortune with interstate and international visitors.

Above: *Perth city centre, seen over one of the lakes of the Narrows Interchange, which lies between Mounts Bay Road and the Swan River.*
Below: *A view of Perth city centre and the eastern suburbs, with the Darling Escarpment in the distance, the Swan River lower right, and the Swan Bells centre right.*

Above: *Looking over the Swan River and Old Perth Port to the Swan Bells at Barrack Square. The green space at centre left is part of The Esplanade, while the trees at centre right grow in Supreme Court Gardens.*

PERTH – CAPITAL OF WESTERN AUSTRALIA

Once, the Nyungar Aboriginal people lived well in the area now known as the Swan River valley. The first British settlers, under the leadership of Captain James Stirling, arrived in 1829. Growth of the colony was steady but slow; progress accelerated with the help of convict labour from 1850 to 1868. In 1885, gold was discovered at Halls Creek in the Kimberley Division, then, in 1892, fabulous strikes were made at Coolgardie and Kalgoorlie, the centre of today's Goldfields region. Gold brought riches and people from many nations to the colony, ensuring its continuing prosperity and development.

In the second half of the twentieth century, wealth from Pilbara iron, Goldfields nickel, Kimberley diamonds and other minerals underwrote the construction of today's Perth. A city of shining modern towers interspersed with beautifully restored old buildings, shady with trees, bright with green spaces and flower gardens, it stands on the banks of the Swan River. A Mediterranean climate of cool, rainy winters and warm, dry summers makes outdoor activities, sport and entertainment a way of life.

Above: *A view across Kings Park and the Mitchell Freeway to the Narrows Bridge and South Perth, from where the Kwinana Freeway runs along the Swan River towards the entrance of the Canning River at top right. Perth Water is at centre left.*

THE BEAUTIFUL SWAN RIVER

The Swan River flows from the Darling Range escarpment to the Indian Ocean across a wide and fertile valley. It runs through farming country and then suburbs before widening into Perth Water and dividing the city. Downstream, it is joined by the Canning River, and eventually enters the Indian Ocean at Fremantle, 19 kilometres from Perth. The Swan is the people's river. Bordered by green lawns, sports grounds, gardens and picnic areas, it is the haunt of sailors, anglers, cyclists and walkers. On the city foreshore, in Barrack Square, stands the Swan Bells, an impressive glass tower housing the historic bells of St Martins-in-the-Fields augmented to make an 18-bell peal, and a display of bells from many different cultures.

Top: *(Left) Catamarans on the Swan River with the city in the background. (Right) The tower of the Swan Bells houses a working peal of 18 bells.*
Above: *(Left) Pleasure craft moored in Matilda Bay, Crawley, with Perth's city towers behind. (Right) Families picnicking beside the Swan River.*
Below: *The paddlewheeler ferry Decoy at rest on the calm surface of the Swan River.*

Above: (Left) Pedestrians in Hay Street Mall, with Perth Town Hall in the background. (Top right) The restored Palace Hotel contrasts with the Bank West tower behind it. (Above right) Murray Street Mall. **Below:** (Left to right) Forrest House, the reconstructed residence of Alexander Forrest, pioneer explorer; Perth Town Hall with broad arrows echoing the brand on the uniforms of convicts who began its construction in 1867; a window in Forrest Chase Shopping Centre; Old Perth Boys School, built between 1852 and 1854.

PERTH CITY SCENES

It is easy to drive, or to take a bus or train into Perth city. Once there, it is well worth exploring the shopping possibilities in the compact city centre. Hay Street and Murray Street Malls and the arcades joining them are full of boutiques and stores, while London Court (built in the 1930s in imitation of a Tudor street) offers specialty shops galore. Northbridge, over the railway line, is known for its restaurants. Perth has a vital cultural life, boasting the world-class Art Gallery of Western Australia, an outstanding Museum, many smaller galleries, and active theatre and music scenes. The Festival of Perth is an internationally respected multi-arts event.

Above: *(Left and right) A shoppers paradise – London Court, a mock-Tudor laneway built in 1937.*
Below: *(Left) The forecourt of the Art Gallery of Western Australia. (Right) The statue of Peter Pan in Queens Gardens.*

Top: (Left) Herdsman Lake is 7 km north-west of the city centre. (Right) The Burswood Hotel, Convention Centre and Casino complex and Golf Course beside the Swan River.
Above: (Left) A bronze Orang-utan and baby welcome visitors to Perth Zoo. (Right) Bronze kangaroos hop across the corner of St Georges Terrace and Barrack Street.
Below: (Left) Elegant residential development at Claisebrook, East Perth. (Right) The WACA, scene of hard-fought sporting fixtures, with the Causeway crossing the river behind.

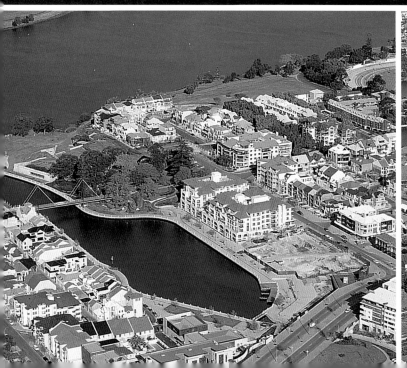

Top: (Left) "The Strike", by Greg James, in front of Perth Mint, Australia's oldest operating mint, established in 1899. (Right) Winthrop Hall, the impressive centrepiece of the University of Western Australia, Crawley.
Above: (Left) Lakeside Shopping Centre, Joondalup. (Right) West Coast TAFE College, Joondalup.

A VIBRANT, VITAL CITY

Perth stands on a coastal plain decorated with beautiful freshwater lakes that have become features in an urban landscape stretching north past Joondalup, west to the Darling Scarp and south past Fremantle. The city treasures its history – a special drawcard is Perth Mint, Australia's longest-operating mint, opened in 1899 as a branch of Britain's Royal Mint. Perth's climate and facilities encourage sporting activities – the WACA (Western Australian Cricket Association) ground and the Esplanade, bordering the Swan River, are famous venues. Weekends are for outdoor fun. A favourite excursion for families is to ride the ferry across the Swan River and visit Perth Zoo, where the major exhibits feature African, Asian and Australian environments and their inhabitants, and where concerts are often held in the evenings.

KINGS PARK

Perth's premier tourist destination, and its local favourite, is Kings Park. It comprises 400 hectares overlooking Perth and the Swan River; about two-thirds is natural bushland. The Western Australian Botanic Garden presents magnificent wildflower displays all year around, climaxing in September's Wildflower Festival. Kings Park, with its stately war memorial and commemorative avenues, excellent restaurant, walking paths and spacious lawns, is a great place to picnic, cycle or stroll. Here it is possible to come close to nature while being just an easy walk from the heart of a modern city.

Top: *A view of Perth city centre across one of the wildflower gardens that border the Swan River section of Kings Park.*
Above: *(Left) The Floral Clock, with Frasers Restaurant at far right. (Right) The Flame of Remembrance and War Memorial.*

Top: *(Left to right)* *Red and Green Kangaroo Paw* (Anigozanthos manglesii) *and Purple Tassels* (Sowerbaea laxiflora); *Splendid White Spider Orchid* (Caladenia splendens); *Many-flowered Fringe Lily* (Thysanotus multiflorus); *Mottlecah* (Eucalyptus macrocarpa).
Above: *(Left and right)* A floral fantasy and an Australian Cottage Garden, on show at Kings Park's annual Wildflower Festival.
Below: *(Left)* The summit of the DNA Tower gives the brave a fine view over Perth's suburbs. *(Right)* A wealth of wildflowers.

Above: *Cottesloe, a favourite family surf beach, has a grassed and shady picnic area, excellent restaurants and cafés, a golf course and a stone groyne that attracts anglers.*
Below: *A view from Scarborough Beach southwards along Floreat and City beaches. Observation City stands tall above the neighbouring buildings.*

Top: *Hillarys Boat Harbour and Sorrento Quay offer a marina, the Aquarium of Western Australia, eateries and safe beaches.*
Above: *(Left to right) Fun at Sorrento Beach; at AQWA, the Aquarium of Western Australia; craft at Mindarie Keys Marina.*

PERTH'S SILVER BEACHES

A glorious line of surf beaches runs north from Fremantle's Port Beach past Perth to Mullaloo. Famous names include Cottesloe, Swanbourne, City, Floreat, Scarborough and Trigg. Still further north is the Hillarys Boat Harbour–Sorrento Quay complex, where AQWA (the Aquarium of Western Australia) is a major attraction. All these beaches are easily accessed from city and suburbs, and are ideal places to relax on the sand or in the water. Many are known for their cafés and restaurants.

FREMANTLE – THE PORT CITY

On the mouth of the Swan River, 19 kilometres from Perth, Fremantle has been described as the world's best-preserved nineteenth-century seaport. Since 1829, the local limestone has provided construction material for a wealth of sturdy and elegant buildings, 150 of which are now classified by the National Trust. Many were built by convicts. The Round House, Fremantle Prison, the Maritime Museum and the Fremantle Arts Centre (once a lunatic asylum) enthral their many visitors. Still a major port, Fremantle is also a base for fishing fleets, a university city and a centre for the arts. It has always been a multicultural city and the many superb restaurants and bistros show various ethnic influences. Any Fremantle experience has to include a visit to the Fremantle Markets, followed by a coffee on South Terrace, or a lunch of fresh-caught seafood at the Fishing Boat Harbour.

Above: *A view of Fremantle across Bathers Bay, past the Round House (built as a prison in 1831) and up High Street. The tunnel beneath the Round House was built by a whaling company in 1837 to provide access to the beach.*

Above: A seagull's-eye-view of maritime Fremantle, across Success Harbour and the Fishing Boat Harbour.
Below: (Clockwise from top left) Fremantle Town Hall and a tram on its scenic tour; the Maritime Museum; seafood restaurants at Fishing Boat Harbour; Fremantle Municipality Council Chambers; the historic P & O building; enjoying the Cappuccino Strip, South Terrace.

Above: *Porpoise Bay on Rottnest is a wonderful place to swim or explore underwater reefs.*
Below: *(Left) Quokkas are common on Rottnest but rare on the mainland. (Right) The lighthouse on Wadjemup Hill.*

ROTTNEST ISLAND

Cut off from the mainland by rising sea level about 7000 years ago, Rottnest Island lies 18 kilometres west of Fremantle. Its coast, which alternates limestone headlands and sandy coves, is surrounded by shallow coral reefs, and fishing, swimming and diving are popular with many of the island's visitors. Others may prefer to walk trails leading to places of interest, or cycle around the roads (few motor vehicles exist on Rottnest). This marvellous holiday destination is popular with nature lovers and with families, whose children find endless fascination in the small wallabies called Quokkas.

Above: *A view across Pinky Beach and Bathurst Light to the settlement at Thompson Bay.*
Below: *Holiday villas on Geordie Bay blend into their environment.*

Above: *The famous limestone Pinnacles at Nambung National Park lie between sand dunes and an area of darker pillars called the Tombstones.*
Below: *(Left) A close-up showing how the Pinnacles are eroded by windblown sand. (Right) Wildflowers on the coastal plains at Coalseam Conservation Park.*

Travelling north of Perth, the Brand Highway more-or-less parallels the coast until it reaches the port of Geraldton. It passes through coastal heathlands and sandy plains that become kaleidoscopes of colour when good winter rains encourage springtime wildflowers. A popular detour westwards is to the remarkable Pinnacles in Nambung National Park.

The Great Northern Highway leads north-north-east from Perth, through the heart of the northern Wheatbelt. On the way, 132 kilometres from Perth, is New Norcia, established as a Spanish Benedictine mission in 1846, and still housing Benedictine monks, as well as a notable museum and art gallery.

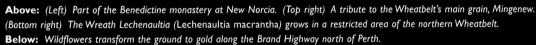

Above: *(Left) Part of the Benedictine monastery at New Norcia. (Top right) A tribute to the Wheatbelt's main grain, Mingenew. (Bottom right) The Wreath Lechenaultia* (Lechenaultia macrantha) *grows in a restricted area of the northern Wheatbelt.*
Below: *Wildflowers transform the ground to gold along the Brand Highway north of Perth.*

Capital of the "Batavia Coast", Geraldton is home to a multi-million-dollar rock lobster fleet. It is the port nearest the Houtman Abrolhos, coral islands on which the tragic drama of the shipwreck of the Dutch East India Company vessel *Batavia* was played out in 1629.

North of Geraldton, a detour westwards from the North West Highway leads through the spectacular scenery of Kalbarri National Park. The Murchison River has carved rugged gorges through rocks known as Tumblagooda Sandstone, laid down 400 million years ago and containing many fossils. The surrounding plains become wildflower gardens from mid-July to early October.

Top: (Left) The Customs House, Geraldton. (Right) Geraldton, a popular holiday resort and cray-fishing port.
Above: (Left) A nineteenth-century building in Greenough Historical Hamlet. (Right) Geraldton Wax (Chamelaucium uncinatum).
Below: Massive rocks and fragile wildflowers in Coalseam Conservation Park, a small reserve north of Mingenew.

Above: *Nature's Window, eroded from the Tumblagooda Sandstone to form a frame for the Murchison River in Kalbarri National Park.*
Below: *The Murchison River and a section of Kalbarri National Park seen over Hawks Head Lookout.*

Top: *The Zuytdorp Cliffs, scene of historic shipwrecks, stretch north along the coast from beyond Kalbarri to Shark Bay.*
Above: *The North West Coastal Highway runs inland through red sand dune country.*

SHARK BAY

Shark Bay is a World Heritage Area, which is famous for its waters and the creatures that live in them, including endangered Dugongs. Bottlenose Dolphins have, since 1960, been coming into the shallows at Monkey Mia to interact with the fascinated crowds. The stromatolites of Hamelin Pool are living examples of a lifeform that existed 3.5 billion years ago. The Peron Peninsula and nearby islands are sanctuaries for rare animals. In Project Eden, the Western Australian Department of Conservation and Land Management aims to reintroduce species of mammals that are on the brink of extinction to an area of Francois Peron National Park that will be kept clear of feral cats and foxes.

Above: *Kangaroo tracks stamp a sand dune where the red sand of the peninsula meets the silver sand of the sea in Francois Peron National Park.*
Below: *(Left) A Bottlenose Dolphin greets admirers at Monkey Mia. (Right) The endangered Rufous Hare-Wallaby (Mala) may be re-established on the Peron Peninsula.*

Top: *(Left) Tall Mulla Mulla,* Ptilotus exaltatus. *(Centre) Sturt's Desert Pea,* Swainsona formosa. *(Right) Poverty Bush,* Eremophila christopheri.
Above: *(Left) Wattle,* Acacia sp. *(Right) Spinifex,* Triodia sp., *and Cotton Bush,* Ptilotus obovatus.
Below: *Flowers on a north-western plain in springtime after good rain has fallen.*

DESERT SURVIVALISTS

Western Australia has one of the richest floras known, the South Western Botanical Province alone supporting over 9000 species of plants. Many groups of plants are adapted to growing on poor soil and in arid regions; often their nectar-rich flowers are pollinated with the help of birds, insects and small mammals. Each spring the floral display begins in the north-west of the State, then spreads southwards and along the southern coast in scenes of great beauty.

The State's native animals are equally hardy. Many inland species are adapted to survive long periods of drought, reproducing when good rains bring renewed life to the desert.

Top: *(Left) The Euro is a wallaroo that lives in arid and rocky habitats. (Right) The Wedge-tailed Eagle is a desert predator.*
Above: *(Left) The Sand Monitor makes its home in a burrow. (Right) The Dingo may hunt on its own or in a family pack.*

Clockwise from top: *Mt Augustus (Burringurrah) is a huge body of rock strata that covers almost 5000 ha – twice the area of Uluṟu; wildflowers in Mt Augustus National Park; the Gascoyne River offers shade and cool water in an arid landscape; the ancient sandstone escarpment of the Kennedy Range.*

THE GASCOYNE AND NORTH WEST CAPE

Carnarvon, the next big town north of Shark Bay on the North West Coastal Highway, is noted for producing tropical fruit irrigated with subsurface water. Carnarvon stands at the mouth of the Gascoyne River, and is a good base for exploring Kennedy Range National Park and the world's largest rock, Mt Augustus. About 370 kilometres further north, near the tip of North West Cape, is the town of Exmouth. Ningaloo Marine Park protects the coastal waters from Bundegi Reef north to the Cape and around it into Exmouth Gulf. In some places, coral reefs are only a few metres from the shoreline and the area is a wonderland of marine life. Rugged Cape Range National Park extends down the spine of North West Cape.

This is an area of gorges and breakaways, harsh and unforgiving country that holds some of the least publicised and dramatic aridland scenery in Australia, but within a short distance of coral reefs that rival the Great Barrier Reef for impact and richness.

Top: *(Left) Travellers gather in the caravan park at North West Cape to enjoy Ningaloo Marine Park. (Right) An aerial view of Cape Range National Park.*
Above: *Yardie Creek Gorge, Cape Range National Park, where salt water is held back from the ocean by a sand bar.*
Below: *(Left) Pink Anemonefish frequent Ningaloo's coral reefs. (Right) Vlamingh Head Lighthouse, North West Cape, overlooks Ningaloo.*

The Pilbara is one of the hottest, and most beautiful, places on earth. It is a land of ancient rocks, many of them rich in iron. This mineral wealth has attracted mining ventures; they have produced both company towns that can accommodate visitors and a network of roads, which make it possible to journey comfortably through desert studded with spinifex and termite mounds to reach red ranges that hide oases of greenery and rock-surrounded water. Karijini National Park, second largest reserve in the State, protects the magnificent scenery of the Hamersley Range.

In this quintessentially Australian landscape, newer mining centres such as Tom Price, Karratha and Paraburdoo contrast with older towns such as Cossack, a port for nineteenth-century pearlers, and Roebourne, which serviced Whim Creek, once noted for its copper mine.

Above: *Fortescue Falls plunge into Dales Gorge in Karijini National Park, which covers over 600 000 ha of the Hamersley Plateau.*

Top: (Left) Dramatic Weano Gorge in Karijini National Park. (Right) Banded Jasper on the Coongan River at Marble Bar, one of Earth's hottest places.
Above: (Left to right) A Heritage building in Cossack; Roebourne Post Office; one of the gigantic trucks used by the Pilbara iron ore mines.
Below: Sunset on Eighty Mile Beach, on the way north to Broome.

カゴシマ県川辺郡
故鮫島久義墓
昭和六年三月二十九日
行年十八才

Top left and clockwise: *Vividly coloured rocks at Gantheaume Point, which ends the long sweep of Cable Beach, 7 km south of Broome; a gravestone at the Japanese Cemetery stands memorial to the old-time pearling days; at Cape Villaret; camel-riding along Cable Beach at day's end.*
Below: *(Left) A window to the sea, Gantheaume Point. (Right) Enjoying the sun, sand and sea at Cable Beach.*

Top: *The coast of the Kimberleys is rugged country, one of the final great areas of wilderness left on Earth.*
Above: *The Saltwater Crocodile lives on Kimberley coasts and in estuaries. (Right) An ideal base for Kimberley fishing.*

THE KIMBERLEY COAST

Since the Kimberley is tropical monsoon country, it is most comfortable and easiest to travel in the cooler part of the dry season, from May until September. Broome, the southern gateway to this final Australian frontier, was once a pearling centre – memories of the boom days, as well as cultured pearls and pearl-shell, are still found there. Visitors can also take a camel ride along stunning Cable Beach, or go to see dinosaur footprints. Further north, the beaches become less frequent and the mangrove swamps and mudflats more common. Inlets lead between cliffs 300 metres high, and the enormous difference between high and low water creates tidal races that swirl through narrow coastal gorges. Exploration of the northern coast, by boat or by plane, reveals pristine wilderness.

Above: *Mitchell Falls, a spectacular series of four cascades on the Mitchell Plateau, 70 km off the Gibb River–Kalumburu road.*

THE WEST KIMBERLEY

The Aboriginal people who had lived in the Kimberley for tens of thousands of years bravely opposed the coming of pastoralists. Places such as Windjana Gorge and Tunnel Creek, in the Napier Range, are rich in memories of their resistance. The history of the Napier Range itself goes back 350 million years, to a time when it was a barrier reef formed under a primeval sea. In more recent times, the Fitzroy River has cut through the range to form Geikie Gorge, and the Lennard River has carved out Windjana Gorge. In the summer Wet, huge volumes of water travel through these gorges then spread out over the rivers' floodplains. Wildlife and domestic stock feast, birds and other wild creatures breed, and the land renews itself, ready to endure the conditions of the Dry.

Top: (Left) An aerial view of the Lennard River. (Right) Windjana Gorge has been carved into the Napier Range by the Lennard River.

Above: Geikie Gorge was formed when the Fitzroy River cut through limestone laid down as a reef under an ancient sea.

Below: Boab trees lose their leaves in the winter Dry and become cloaked in green in the Wet. (Right) Bell Creek, in Bell Gorge, is an oasis in the West Kimberley ranges.

Above: *The 350-million-years-old Bungle Bungles, properly called Purnululu, are rounded domes of striking but fragile rock. This pool is in Piccaninny Gorge.*
Below: *(Left) Unique palm trees grow in Echidna Chasm, in the north of Purnululu. (Right) A close-up shows the stripes of orange silica and darker lichen that band the domes.*

The Great Northern Highway passes to the south of the Napier Range, pauses at Fitzroy Crossing and then begins the long run north-east, through the historic goldrush town of Halls Creek and past Purnululu National Park to Kununurra and Wyndham. Much of the country is grassy plainland sprinkled with Boab trees and termite mounds. The effort needed to reach Purnululu National Park is well worth making. The park protects the Bungle Bungles – dome-like, banded formations of sandstone that look as if they were built to last forever, but which are, in reality, fragile and easily eroded. The fascinating bands are formed by strata of harder rock covered with iron and manganese that alternate with more porous bands where retained water fosters the growth of dark-hued algae.

Top: (Left) China Wall, a vein of quartz just east of Halls Creek. **Above:** Mustering cattle across the Fitzroy River plains. **Below:** (Left) This statue at Halls Creek commemorates Russian Jack, a character of the 1885 goldrush, who carried a sick mate over 300 km in his wheelbarrow. (Right) Turkey Creek is the only settlement between Halls Creek and Kununurra.

Above: *(Left) A poppet head crowns the Federal Hotel in Kalgoorlie, the capital of the Goldfields.*
Top right: *Camels hauled goods to the goldrush towns. These haughty beasts stand in Norseman, south of Kalgoorlie.*
Above right: *The Palace Hotel, Norseman, was established in 1907.*

WHEATBELT AND GOLDFIELDS

Western Australia's Wheatbelt forms a long, thin triangle with its apex near Geraldton in the north and its southern base stretching from Cranbrook all the way east to Ravensthorpe. Much of the native bush has been cleared for cereal-growing and stock-raising, but in many places farmers have been frustrated by massive granite outcrops called tors. One such tor forms Wave Rock, near Hyden. Dryandra Woodlands Reserve, near Narrogin, protects the endangered Numbat.

The Goldfields lies further east still. Centres such as Coolgardie, Kalgoorlie–Boulder and Norseman were the scenes of fabulous strikes just over a century ago, and gold and nickel are still mined. This is desert country, home to remarkable plants and animals that thrive in the arid conditions.

Top left and clockwise: *A farmer and his sheep dogs, near Wagin; a wool wagon at Kojonup pays tribute to the sheep farmed on many Wheatbelt properties; a relic of the pioneer days at Arthur River; the woolly wealth of the Wheatbelt.*
Below: *(Left) Wave Rock, a granite crest near Hyden. (Right) The endangered Numbat is being conserved at Dryandra Woodland Reserve.*

Above: *Busselton's two-kilometre jetty was built in many stages over 95 years. Several sections of the promenade were destroyed by a cyclone in 1978.*
Below: *(Left) Cape Leeuwin Lighthouse. (Right) The lighthouse on Cape Naturaliste.*
Bottom: *(Left) Sugarloaf Rock, near Cape Naturaliste, is a popular place to watch seabirds. (Right) Bunbury's Regional Art Galleries are housed in an elegant building, once a convent.*

Top: *(Left) Margaret River is famous for its wines, and visitors are welcome for tours and tastings. This is Brookland Valley Winery.*
Above: *Stalagmites in Mammoth Cave, between Capes Naturaliste and Leeuwin. (Right) A welcoming faun, Margaret River.*

PERTH TO CAPE LEEUWIN

South of Perth, the South Western Highway runs past coastal inlets and through Jarrah and Tuart forests to Bunbury and Busselton, ports with fascinating histories, that are now popular holiday resorts.

Leeuwin–Naturaliste National Park stretches almost the entire length of the coastline between these two Capes. The area offers magnificent coastal scenery, a cave system that has produced fossils of prehistoric creatures and the outliers of the majestic Karri forests. Margaret River, the central town of the Leeuwin coast, is noted for award-winning wineries, restaurants, artists' enclaves and some of Australia's most notable surf breaks.

Great Southern towns such as Pemberton and Manjimup, once dedicated to logging the tall forests, are now places for visitors to stay while exploring those same forests. Warren, Beedelup and Shannon National Parks are sanctuaries where tall trees and rushing forest streams can be seen close-up. The towering Karri, which may reach 90 metres in height, is not the only tall tree of the region. In the Valley of the Giants, Walpole–Nornalup National Park, four species of rare eucalypts grow in a small area and those visitors with heads for heights can view the forest canopy from an elevated walkway.

Along the south coast, D'Entrecasteaux National Park merges into Walpole–Nornalup. These are places to walk, enjoy the ocean, fish and revel in nature's glories. William Bay National Park, just west of Denmark, includes the lovely cove called Greens Pool and the granite Elephant Rocks. The Bibbulmun Walking Track, which leads from Kalamunda, near Perth, ends in Denmark.

Top: (Left) Amongst the giant Tingle trees of the Valley of the Giants. (Right) A forest giant.
Above: (Left) Historic steam engine at Pemberton, a major timber town. (Right) Viewing the canopy in the Valley of the Giants.

Top: *(Left) Elephant Rocks, granite boulders in William Bay National Park. (Right) The lower reaches of the Denmark River.*
Above: *At Green Pool, a superb stretch of coastal scenery in William Bay National Park.*
Below: *(Left) The green and pleasant country near Nannup. (Right) In Wilson Inlet, near Denmark, the local pelicans wait for their share of the catch.*

Above: *(Left) A maritime memento in front of the Town Hall, York Street, Albany. (Right) Whaleworld, at Frenchmans Bay Road, exhibits the beached whale chaser, Cheynes IV.*
Below: *(Left) The Gap, carved by the ocean from the granite of Torndirrup National Park. (Right) Two Peoples Bay, a nature reserve that harbours rare birds and mammals.*

Above: *Natural Bridge, a massive span of granite boulders in Torndirrup National Park.*

GRANDEUR IN GRANITE

Albany was settled in 1826 to forestall French colonisation. It became a whaling port, a coaling station for steamships and a shipping centre for farm produce. The town stands on Princess Royal Harbour and is protected from the Southern Ocean by a rugged granite coastline that alternates stark and dramatic headlands and precipitous cliffs with sheltered bays. This area is included in Torndirrup National Park, while Cheyne Beach Whaling Station in Frenchmans Bay preserves memories of the whaling era, which ended in 1978. The sandy heathlands that fringe the southern beaches support a rich variety of wildlife, including several endangered species, and are wildflower gardens in spring.

Top left and clockwise: *Custard Orchid,* Thelymitra villosa; *Scarlet Banksia,* Banksia coccinea; *flowering heathland and the Stirling Range; Hood-leaved Hakea,* Hakea cucullata; *Cats Paw,* Anigozanthos onycis; *Cranbrook Bell,* Darwinia meeboldii.

THE STIRLING RANGE

Just on 76 kilometres north of Albany, the Stirling Range towers above the surrounding heathland and farmland. The highest point, Bluff Knoll, rises to just over 1000 metres. The area contains over 1500 species of plants, 82 of which are found nowhere else. Some peaks have their own distinct populations of wildflowers. This is wonderful country to walk, provided precautions are taken against sudden weather changes. "Dieback", a fungus lethal to native plants, is a problem here and in many other south-western and southern reserves. Visitors are asked to assist in efforts to control it.

Above: *A flock of White-tailed Black-Cockatoos flies across farmland at the foot of the Stirling Range.*
Below: *(Left) Mt Magog and other Stirling peaks consist of sandstone, quartzite and shales. (Right) Bluff Knoll, whose Aboriginal name is Pualaar Miial, is 1073 m high.*

Above: *Cape Arid National Park lies at the western end of the Great Australian Bight, on the fringes of the Nullarbor Plain.*
Below: *(Left) Stilts and gulls in a watercourse, Fitzgerald River National Park. (Right) The Royal Hakea, Hakea victoria, is found only in Fitzgerald River National Park and in parts of the nearby Ravensthorpe Range.*

THE SOUTH-EAST COAST

From Albany the South Coast Highway runs along the shoreline, then turns inland to skirt the northern boundary of Fitzgerald River National Park before reaching the town of Esperance. This coastal resort has been in turn a goldrush port, a pastoral town and, most recently, a delightful place to stay while visiting five national parks – Cape Le Grand, Rossiter Bay, Cape Arid, Stokes Inlet and, to the north, Peak Charles.

Strollers on Esperance's picturesque jetty can be prepared to see Sammy the Sea-lion (or one of his relatives) in the water below. These sleek swimmers breed on nearby islands and frequent Esperance Bay: a bronze statue advertises the local fondness for them.

Top left and clockwise: *Australian Sea-lions can be seen swimming in Esperance Bay and even under the town jetty; the statue of "Sammy Sea-lion" on the Esperance waterfront; Esperance is the port for cattle and crops and a holiday resort for the Goldfields (the name "Esperance" was taken from a French ship that sheltered in the bay in 1792); Esperance Jetty.*